WELCOME TO CORGARFF CASTLE

On first seeing Corgarff Castle in its lonely moorland setting, the visitor might mistake it for a castle much like any other. But this impression is soon dispelled by the distinctive star-shaped perimeter wall that surrounds the little tower.

Corgarff's story is really two stories. The first takes us from the middle of the 16th century, when the tower was built, through to the close of the 17th century, when it was abandoned. This period was the castle's heyday, when it served as the impressive fortified home of the Forbeses of Corgarff.

The second takes us from the mid-18th century, when the tower was turned into soldiers' barracks, through to 1831, when the British army no longer had a use for this remote base. In that time, the redcoats based in the old tower patrolled Strathdon, hunting down Jacobite sympathisers. Latterly they helped the excisemen stamp out the illegal production and smuggling of whisky.

Above: A glimpse of the castle through one of the gunloops in the perimeter wall.

Opposite: A redcoat's tunic hangs in the reconstructed barrack room on the second floor.

CONTENTS

CORGARFF CASTLE AT A GLANCE

The original castle, built around 1550 and occupied by a branch of Clan Forbes, was typical of small houses of the 16th-century Scottish gentry. The nucleus was the tower house. The main living room, the hall, was on the first floor, with a basement for storage below and private chambers above. Around the tower house, within a stout courtyard wall, would have been other buildings, including a stable, bakehouse and brewhouse.

Opposite: A painting of the castle by James Giles, dated 1831, the year the castle was abandoned by the military.

After the Battle of Culloden in 1746, the tower house was transformed into barracks for a garrison of government soldiers stationed in northern Scotland. The high, stone-vaulted ceiling of the old hall was removed and an extra timber floor inserted. Outside, the courtyard buildings and wall were demolished and replaced by two single-storey pavilions and the star-shaped perimeter wall, studded with musket loops, which gives Corgarff its unrivalled appearance.

CHANGING ROLES

6   A LORDLY RESIDENCE
Corgarff was originally built around 1550, as a modest-sized but comfortable tower-house for the Forbes family.

20 A JACOBITE RALLYING POINT
The castle became an important base for the Jacobites during the Risings of 1715 and 1745–6.

10 A MILITARY BARRACKS
After Culloden, the castle underwent significant adaptation to become a base for government forces.

DISTINCTIVE FEATURES

13 THE PERIMETER WALL
The star-shaped wall surrounding the castle was added in the late 1740s.

6   THE BOX-MACHICOLATION
The most obvious vestige of Corgarff's original defences is the remnant of an overhanging structure above the main entrance.

6   THE EXTERNAL STAIR
The stone entrance stairway was added in the 1740s, but the entrance to the castle was always at first-floor level.

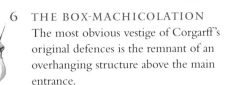

MEMORABLE EVENTS

18 A TERRIBLE MASSACRE
In 1571, 24 people were killed when raiders set fire to Corgarff.

21 AN ABANDONED STRONGHOLD
In March 1746, 400 redcoats struggled through snow and icy winds to oust Jacobite forces from Corgarff. They arrived to find a cat the only remaining resident.

28 A WHISKY BUSINESS
After years controlling illegal stills, Corgarff became a licensed distillery in 1826.

BLEAK SURROUNDINGS

26 THE MILITARY ROAD AND BRIDGES
Around 1750, a new military road was built which linked Corgarff to Fort George in the north and Blairgowrie in the south. Much of it survives and parts can be found near the castle.

31 LOCAL RESIDENTS
Photographic displays in the castle show some of the wildlife to be found in the area, including hares, deer and red squirrels.

3

A TOUR OF CORGARFF CASTLE

Corgarff Castle was built as a lordly residence about the middle of the 16th century. Despite the sweeping changes made by the military authorities between 1748 and 1750, enough survives of the original tower house to indicate how it was designed as a residence for the Forbes family. Those features which have not been retained in the fabric have mostly survived in technical drawings made in 1748 by the Board of Ordnance, the body responsible for converting the lordly castle into barracks.

Illustration key

1. Tower house
2. West pavilion
3. East pavilion
4. Perimeter wall
5. Entrance

Photos, left to right:
The perimeter wall's main entrance; the old cistern in the courtyard; a basement cellar; George III fireplace; remains of the box machicolation.

THE CASTLE OF THE FORBES FAMILY

The rectangular tower house was modest in size compared to most Scottish tower houses built in the later 16th century. It measured 12m by 8m and stood to a height of almost 15m. It contained three floors and a garret, arranged in the conventional manner of the period: storage in the basement, the hall on the first floor, and private chambers above. All the floors were linked by a single stone spiral stair which occupied the same position as the present timber stair, the SE corner. The stone steps spiralled around a stone column called a newel. One newel stone is still visible in the window recess behind the steward's desk in the first-floor room, where it has been re-used as a building material.

THE ENTRANCE DOORWAY

The tower house was entered at first-floor level. The present external stone stair was added by the military. The original access stair may have been timber.

Directly above the entrance doorway, on the outside near the wall-top, stone corbels still project out from the wall. These once formed part of a small overhanging defence, called a box-machicolation, from which the occupants could defend the door, the weakest part of the tower.

THE BASEMENT

The basement was divided into two stone-vaulted cellars, both of them cool and dimly lit by narrow window slits. These held the main provisions for the laird and his family. Further storage space was available in buildings outside the tower.

Left: The corbels that once supported a box-machicolation defence above the main door.

Right: The castle as it would have looked around 1600.

THE HALL AND KITCHEN

The first floor was divided into two rooms. The larger of these was the hall, the main living space in the tower, which has now lost much of its grandeur. After taking over the building in 1748, the military authorities removed its original high stone-vaulted ceiling to squeeze in an extra floor, and narrowed the original fireplace in the west wall. The original hall, with its generous windows and fireplace, must have presented an imposing spectacle.

The smaller room served as the kitchen. It originally had a large fireplace in the east wall and a slop-drain (still visible) in the north-facing window. This room too had a stone-vaulted ceiling, though not as high as the one over the hall. Instead, there was a little room, also stone-vaulted, above the kitchen. It had a small fireplace, two wall cupboards and a privy in one corner. The wall cupboard to the left of the fireplace had a hidden compartment beneath it, where coin and other valuables could be secretly stored. This little room may have served as the private chamber of the laird's steward, who was responsible for maintaining his master's house and keeping it well provisioned.

Below: A drawing made by the Board of Ordnance in 1748 shows the structure of the castle before it was reconfigured as a barracks.

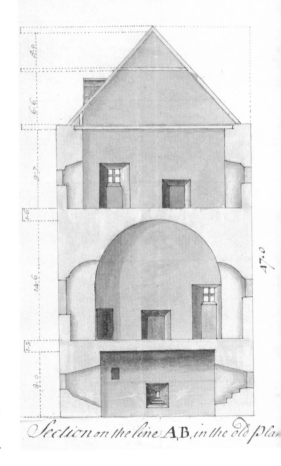

Section on the line A,B, in the old Plan

THE PRIVATE CHAMBERS

The family rooms were located on the upper floors. The floor directly above the hall (now the top floor) was divided into two rooms of roughly equal size. Each had a fireplace and what appear to have been privies in their north walls. These rooms formed the private apartment of the laird and his lady – a withdrawing room and bed chamber. The two rooms in the garret at the top provided additional chambers for other members of the family and servants.

Above: A view of the castle from the SW. A vestige of the original box-machicolation is visible just below the roof.

Below: The cistern is one of the few features that survive from the original tower house.

OUTSIDE THE TOWER HOUSE

The tower house never stood alone, but would have been surrounded by other buildings – including a stable and other service offices such as a bakehouse and brewhouse. These would have been grouped around a courtyard, and enclosed within a defensive wall. However, these were swept away by the military in 1748. The plans drawn up by the Board of Ordnance refer to two huts abutting the tower house, which confirms the presence of other structures. Possibly the only original feature now surviving is the water cistern in the courtyard.

THE TOWER HOUSE CONVERTED

The work undertaken for the Board of Ordnance between 1748 and 1750 saw the 200-year-old tower house converted into soldiers' barracks. Only the basement was left largely unaltered: the two cellars continued in use as stores for food, drink and military supplies.

The rest of the tower house was completely gutted. The most radical change was the complete removal of the stone-vaulted ceiling over the hall, and the insertion of an additional floor. The resulting space provided sleeping accommodation for the commanding officer, three NCOs and up to 42 men.

THE OFFICER'S ROOM

The main room on the first floor provided accommodation for the commanding officer. This was occupied by Lieutenant Leslie in 1749 and Ensign Rutherford in 1750, and their successors in this isolated command post. The room served as a bedroom, sitting-room and office. From here, the officer would write regular returns and reports to his senior officer based at Braemar Castle, issue orders to his subordinates, and interview prisoners.

Highlanders in the area might be arrested on suspicion of having Jacobite sympathies, of carrying arms or wearing Highland dress (that is, the kilt), and latterly of illegally distilling or smuggling whisky.

The room would have been furnished simply but quite comfortably, in contrast to the rudely-finished and overcrowded barrack rooms on the upper floors.

Left: The uniform worn by 18th-century government troops, known as 'redcoats'.

Right: The castle as it would have looked around 1750.

THE KITCHEN

The smaller room beside the officer's room served as the garrison kitchen. It was subsequently converted, probably in 1827, into a room for a second officer, and a new kitchen was then provided in one of the two pavilions added to the tower house in 1748.

Above: The barrack room reconstruction on the second floor shows the kind of crowded conditions endured by the redcoats.

THE BARRACK ROOMS

The three upper floors were barrack rooms. Board of Ordnance drawings of the time show a crowded maximum provision of eight double beds to each room. The NCOs, one to each barrack room, each had a bed to himself. The privates slept two to a bed, though the intention was that half the small garrison would be out on patrol while the other half slept. Thus, each room was routinely expected to hold 15 men. The space was more than sufficient to house the two NCOs and 21 men stationed here in 1750, and it is likely that the topmost floor was used for storing kit and military equipment, and pressed into use as reserve accommodation only when the need arose. The first barrack room, directly above the officer's room and kitchen, has been reconstructed to show how it would have looked in 1750 when redcoats from Pulteney's 13th Regiment of Foot were in residence under the command of Ensign Rutherford.

THE COURTYARD AND STAR-SHAPED WALL

The cobbled courtyard around the tower house was enclosed within a star-shaped wall, with gun-loops to take the muskets issued to the redcoats. The little barracks was designed to be held against a lightly-armed attacker, but not against cannon. So far as we know, the garrison was never put to the test.

Above: The perimeter wall as shown on a Board of Ordnance plan.

Below: The hostile front presented by the castle to enemies of the Crown.

THE PAVILIONS

Ancillary accommodation for the garrison was provided outside the tower house, in the two single-storey pavilions added to the tower's side walls.

The west pavilion housed the bakehouse and brewhouse. A soldier's basic diet included bread and beer. Both staples were made here and rationed out daily to the men. In addition, each man received a pound of beef a day, occasionally supplemented by cheese, butter and peas. The men cooked for themselves, either in the kitchen or over the grates in their barrack rooms, where they also ate.

The men baked their own bread or oatcakes in the oven provided, but the beer was made by a brewer contracted to come in once a week with his assistant to maintain the stock.

In addition to his daily ration, each man could buy extra, but with his daily pay of a shilling (12 old pence) and beer at two pence a pint there was little room for luxuries.

The east pavilion housed the guardroom and prison. The main function of the small garrison was to police the remote glens of western Aberdeenshire. The redcoats were expected to search out Jacobite sympathisers

Below: The east pavilion and the cobbled courtyard.

and arrest anyone who broke the law. At this time, wearing Highland dress was a crime, as was carrying a weapon. The garrison was also instructed to stamp out the illegal distilling and smuggling of whisky.

All prisoners were held in the castle's prison until they could be escorted under guard to magistrates in Aberdeen or Perth. The magistrate in Inverness was bypassed, as he rarely upheld a prosecution; his sympathies, it was felt, were too much with his fellow Highlanders.

When the army reoccupied the barracks in 1827, the west pavilion became the kitchen and bakehouse, while the east pavilion was converted to a powder store.

Today, the west pavilion has been reconstructed as a small whisky distillery, to show how it may have been used in 1826 when Mr McHardy, who then resided in the tower, obtained a licence to distil whisky. The east pavilion is not normally open to visitors, being reserved for Historic Scotland's steward and storage.

Above: Detail from an engraving by Rev C. Cordiner, probably dating from the 1780s, which shows the castle while it was occupied by the military garrison.

Below: One of the fireplaces used by the redcoats, not only for heating but also for rudimentary cooking.

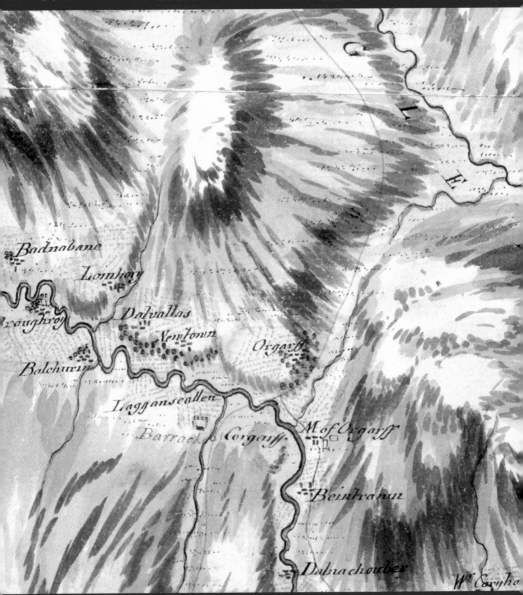

THE STORY OF
CORGARFF CASTLE

SEAT OF THE FORBESES OF TOWIE

Corgarff Castle was built about 1550. However, the builder's identity is unclear. In 1507, the Forest of Corgarff ('forest' in this context meant a hunting reserve) had been granted by James IV to Alexander Elphinstone. He was then residing at Kildrummy Castle, further down Strathdon, and was subsequently created the first Lord Elphinstone. The second Lord Elphinstone made over the Corgarff estate to his eldest son as a marriage gift in 1546. Perhaps the tower was built following this happy event.

Shortly after the marriage, however, the lands of Corgarff were passed to one of Lord Elphinstone's tenants, John Forbes of Towie, an estate near Kildrummy, and it is equally possible that it was he who commissioned the tower house. Strathdon was then one of the wildest and remotest districts of Scotland, and the Forbeses would have required a strong house to protect themselves, their dependants and valuables.

The Forbeses were a powerful Aberdeenshire family who had played a significant part in the Wars of Independence against England, 1296–1357. By 1500, the clan dominated Aberdeenshire and Banffshire from such imposing castles as Druminnor, Tillycairn and Tolquhon. Clan Forbes is renowned for its long-running feud with Clan Gordon, which reached its bloody climax in 1571.

Above: The Forbes coat of arms.

Opposite: Part of William Roy's famous military map of Scotland, which marks Corgarff. The map was made before the new military road was built in 1753–4.

TIMELINE

1271	1507
DUNCAN DE FORBES granted feudal title to the land of Forbes.	JAMES IV grants Forest of Corgarff to Alexander Elphinstone of Kildrummy.

THE MASSACRE OF 1571

The first reference to the castle at Corgarff comes spilling onto the pages of history in the winter of 1571. Following the slaughter of the Gordons at Druminnor Castle, a pitched battle was fought at Tillyangus, in which the Forbeses were routed. Shortly afterwards, the Gordons followed up their victory with a raid on Corgarff.

In November, Adam Gordon, laird of Auchindoun, in Glen Fiddich, over the mountains to the north, came with his men to Corgarff, intent on capturing Forbes of Towie. The laird was away, but his wife Margaret was at home and refused them entry. And so the assailants savagely set fire to the castle, murdering Margaret, her family and servants in the process. In all, 24 people perished in the fire. The massacre is remembered in the old ballad *Edom o' Gordon*.

Above: Druminnor Castle, Aberdeenshire. Bloodshed here provoked the Gordons into terrible revenge at Corgarff.

Opposite: An engraving by Bellenger, published in 1886, takes a rather romantic view of the events of 1571.

An extract from
EDOM O' GORDON

'Set fire to the house!' quo fals Gordon,
All wud [mad] wi dule [distress] and ire:
'Fals lady, ye sall rue this deid
As ye burn in the fire!' …

O then bespake her little son,
Sat on the nurse's knee;
Says, 'Mither dear, gie owre this house,
For the reek [smoke] it smithers me.'

'I wad gie a my gowd [gold], my bairn,
Sae wad I a my fee,
For ae blast o the western wind,
To blaw the reek frae thee.'

O then bespake her dochter dear –
She was baith jimp [slender] and sma:
'O row [wrap] me in a pair o sheets,
And tow me owre the wa!'

They row'd her in a pair o sheets,
And tow'd her owre the wa;
But on the point o Gordon's spear
She gat a deadly fa …

But when the lady saw the fire
Come flaming owre her head,
She wept, and kiss'd her children twain,
Says, 'Bairns, we been but dead.'

Published in *The Oxford Book of Ballads*, edited by Arthur Quiller-Couch, 1910

1546	**1571**		
JOHN FORBES of Towie, tenant of the Elphinstones, acquires Corgarff.	CLAN FORBES AND CLAN GORDON fight a bitter feud.		

CORGARFF AND THE JACOBITES

L ife in Strathdon in the 17th century continued to be dangerous and violent. In 1607, Corgarff was seized and held by a band of local ruffians supported by 'Highland thieves'. Two years later, a gang of Highlanders attacked the stockmen and shepherds of Corgarff and stole their animals.

In 1645, the castle figured once more in national affairs when it was occupied by the Marquis of Montrose, campaigning on behalf of the beleaguered Charles I. In the first Jacobite Rising of 1689–90, it was set ablaze by Jacobite supporters of the exiled Catholic King James VII & II, to deny its use as a garrison post for those supporting the new Protestant sovereigns, William and Mary.

Above: John Erskine, 6th Earl of Mar, who used Corgarff as a rallying point for the third Jacobite Rising in 1715.

By now, the castle was in the ownership of John Erskine, 6th Earl of Mar. In 1715, the Earl launched the third Jacobite Rising from his ancestral seat at Kildrummy Castle, further down Strathdon, then marched to Corgarff to recruit and arm his force, before going on to Braemar to raise the standard for James Edward Stuart, the 'Old Pretender'.

Left: Kildrummy Castle, where the earl began recruiting his Jacobite force.

This incident illustrates Corgarff's peculiar importance. Though fortified, it was certainly no major place of strength. But its secluded position made it an ideal base for fomenting disaffection, which the established government found difficult to counter.

CORGARFF AND THE '45

C orgarff's remoteness was emphasised during the fifth and final Jacobite Rising of 1745–6. In the spring of 1746, the army of Prince Charles Edward, son of the 'Old Pretender', had retired in good order from the English Midlands to the Scottish Highlands. While the Duke of Cumberland advanced slowly up the Scottish east coast at the head of a large government army, the Jacobites took possession of Corgarff, filling it with barrels of gunpowder, muskets and ammunition in preparation for a lengthy war in the mountains.

In late March, a detachment of redcoats – 300 infantry and 100 cavalry, commanded by Lord Ancrum – was despatched from Aberdeen. Their arduous progress, through bitter weather and snowstorms, is described in a letter from one of the officers in the party: 'after a most terrible march … found [Corgarff] abandoned by the garrison, but so lately, that the fire was burning … no living creature in the house but a poor cat sitting by the fire.'

The task of destroying the military stores, begun by the Jacobites before they fled, was completed by the redcoats. Soon afterwards, on 16 April 1746, the Jacobite army itself was defeated at the Battle of Culloden.

Below: Prince Charles Edward Stuart, known as Bonnie Prince Charlie, who led the fifth and final Jacobite Rising of 1745–6.

1645	1715

THE MARQUIS OF MONTROSE occupies Corgarff during his campaigns on behalf of Charles I.

JAMES EDWARD STUART'S standard is raised at Braemar by the Earl of Mar, who uses Corgarff as a recruiting base.

CORGARFF AND THE REDCOATS

After Culloden, the military authorities decided to include western Aberdeenshire in its network of garrisons; hitherto, these had been concentrated in the western and central Highlands.

In the spring of 1748, Lieutenant-Colonel David Watson, deputy quartermaster-general in North Britain, and his civilian surveyor, the 21-year-old William Roy, inspected the castles at Corgarff and Braemar with a view to having them converted into soldiers' barracks. Watson was already busy supervising the rebuilding of mighty Fort Augustus, halfway between Inverness and Fort William, which had been badly damaged by the Jacobites in the build-up to Culloden.

Roy was also employed on another great project, the Military Survey of Scotland, the complete mapping of the country. He did not complete the task until 1755, but in his later army career he laid the foundations for the organisation we now know as the Ordnance Survey.

Opposite (top right): Fort George, the crowning achievement of 18th-century military architecture in the Highlands.

Opposite (centre right): Part of the new network of military roads that connected Corgarff with Fort George and other government bases.

Below: Detail of an illustration from an 18th-century map showing redcoats arresting kilted Jacobites.

While Corgarff and Braemar were being converted into barracks, a new military road was being planned. It would eventually run from Blairgowrie in the south to the new garrison fortress at Fort George, beside the Moray Firth, and would pass close to both Corgarff and Braemar. Braemar subsequently became the main military station, under a captain, while Corgarff's garrison was headed by a subaltern. The date – 1748 – and several sets of initials were recorded on a fireplace lintel on the third floor in the 1920s but are scarcely visible now.

1746

JACOBITE TROOPS

use Corgarff as an arms store.

1746

GOVERNMENT TROOPS

destroy the arms store prior to the Battle of Culloden (left).

PULTENEY'S 13TH FOOT

I n 1750, Ensign Robert Rutherford, serving in General Pulteney's Regiment, the 13th Foot, was at Corgarff in command of a detachment of 45 non-commissioned officers and men, all out-stationed from Fort George. About half of them were out-posted on patrol, either living in hired barns or billeted on a reluctant and frequently hostile local population. A sergeant, a corporal and 21 men remained quartered in the castle along with their commanding officer.

The tense atmosphere in Strathdon in those days is reflected in Rutherford's reports. On 12 October 1750, he wrote: 'one of the soldiers … had his fingers cut very desperately by a fellow in the country on Wednesday last, the soldier says it was because he would not drink the Pretender's health, but the fellow denies that. However, I sent a party, and had him apprehended at night, and he was sent to justice of peace who has order'd him to find bail to stand his trial on Monday next.'

This troubled situation seems not to have prevailed for long. By 1754, Major-General Bland, Commander-in-Chief of George II's forces in Scotland, felt able to write: 'Brae Mar and Corgarff, where we now have two small barracks erected, the good effects of which is now plainly felt by bringing in the people of that barbarous and mountainous country into a

Above: A re-enactment of daily life for a soldier living in Corgarff barracks.

Left: George II, whose entitlement to the thrones of Scotland and England was rejected by the Jacobites. His government responded by establishing a series of military bases in the Highlands.

Opposite (far right): The memorial stone of Nathaniel Forbes, who was born at Corgarff barracks in 1766.

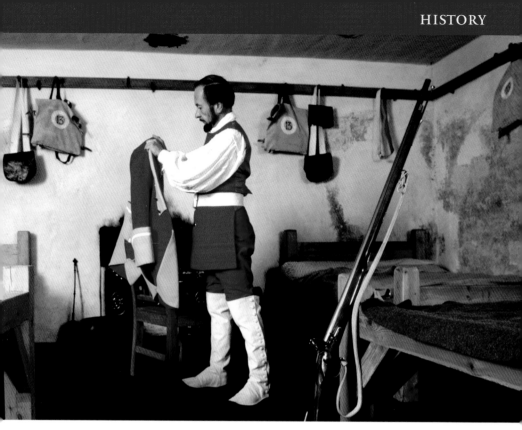

peaceable and orderly state, and they are now become honest and industrious and live with great friendship and amity with His Majesty's troops quartered there.'

On 2 February 1766, Corgarff Castle witnessed the birth of Nathaniel Forbes, whose memorial can be seen in Strathdon Kirk – which suggests that life in the garrison was not altogether bleak.

1748	1750

CORGARFF REFITTED
as a barracks for redcoats.

PULTENEY'S 13TH FOOT
stationed at Corgarff, with 21 men and two NCOs under the command of Ensign Rutherford.

THE MILITARY ROAD

The military road linking Blairgowrie with the garrison fortress of Fort George passes close by Corgarff Castle. It can be followed on foot for about three miles (5km), leaving the A939 about half a mile (1km) east of the castle and continuing west.

This road was constructed between 1749 and 1753, but the road-building campaign began earlier. In the aftermath of the 1715 Jacobite Rising, Major-General George Wade decided that an effective road network was critical to the pacification of the Highland clans. Soon after his arrival in Scotland in 1725, he set in train a massive road-building programme. By the time he left 15 years later, there were over 250 miles of military road winding through the mountains and glens, replacing the dirt tracks of earlier times. Thereafter, his assistant, Major William Caulfield, took over the task. Caulfield oversaw the building of three times as many miles of road, including the Blairgowrie to Fort George highway. He also advised county officials, who were engaged in building roads to encourage economic growth.

Above: A section of the military road near Corgarff Castle.

Below: An inscription at Well of the Lecht records completion of part of the road.

This network of military roads forms the basis of the modern road system in the Highlands. In 1814 responsibility for them passed to the Commissioners appointed under the terms of the Road and Bridges Act of 1812. Many stretches are still in use, including the part running past Corgarff (now the A93 and A939). Some of the bridges also survive as reminders of their labours, notably the fine six-arched Invercauld Bridge over the River Dee NE of Braemar.

The roads were largely built by the soldiers, with specialists from the Board of Ordnance carrying out the survey work and private masonry contractors building the bridges. The work was carried out in the summer months by gangs of up to 500 men, who received double pay for their aches and pains. They were quartered under canvas, in huts and in temporary barracks, retiring to permanent quarters for the winter.

Above: Major-General George Wade, who initiated the road-building programme in the Highlands.

1753

BLAIRGOWRIE TO FORT GEORGE military road opened. It includes the 'Brig o' Dee' (right) at Invercauld, near Braemar.

1814

RESPONSIBILITY for the military roads and bridges turned over to government Commissioners.

CORGARFF AND WHISKY

'We'll mak our maut, and brew our drink,
We'll dance, and sing, and rejoice, man;
And mony thanks to the muckle black De'il
That danced awa wi the Exciseman.'

Robert Burns 'The De'il's Awa wi the Exciseman', 1792

By the end of the 18th century, Corgarff's military importance had faded. The garrison now comprised just two or three Invalids (soldiers disabled on active service or too old to serve in the field) out-posted from the Company of Invalids stationed at Fort George. The castle was even used as a shooting lodge on occasions.

In 1802, Corgarff was returned to private hands, and a local man, James McHardy, rented it as a farmhouse. In 1826 he is recorded as holding a licence permitting him to distil whisky on the premises, but in July of that year his distillery was wilfully set on fire and destroyed. The culprit was never discovered.

The following year, McHardy was asked to vacate the premises so that the army could once again move

in. The redcoats had been posted back to Corgarff to assist the excisemen in a nationwide drive to stamp out the illicit production and smuggling of whisky. This was a highly unpopular campaign: distilling the 'mountain dew' was a time-honoured tradition.

Above: The whisky distillery reconstructed in the west pavilion shows how it might have looked in the days of James McHardy.

Left: Despite the best efforts of the excisemen and the redcoats, illicit stills thrived in the Highlands, as this photograph from around 1900 shows.

Farmer McHardy may have lost the castle, but he did not lose out altogether, for he secured a contract as the garrison's main supplier of provisions – and at prices that reflected a seller's market!

The garrison now consisted of a captain, a subaltern and 56 men from the 25th Regiment of Foot, who assisted the excisemen until 1831. As the larger garrison could not be accommodated in the tower house, a nearby cottage was rented from McHardy to provide space for the barrack-sergeant and a small hospital. This was replaced by a purpose-built structure in 1829.

1827

REDCOATS
REOCCUPY
Corgarff to help stamp out illicit whisky distilling and smuggling.

1831

REDCOATS
LEAVE
Corgarff for the last time.

THE TWILIGHT YEARS

After the garrison finally pulled out in 1831, the castle gradually fell into decay. At first it was occupied by farm workers, and finally by the two Ross sisters, who were still there in 1912.

In 1961, the derelict ruin was entrusted into state care by Sir Edmund and Lady Stockdale, who subsequently assisted in the first phase of preservation work.

Today, the castle steward welcomes visitors from all over the world to this remote stronghold.

Above: The castle in its remote setting.

Below left: The Ross sisters, known as 'the Castle Ladies', were the last residents of the castle.

A WELL POPULATED HABITAT

The castle sits on high ground overlooking Strathdon, where the River Don meanders through pasture and farmland, enclosed by coniferous woodland, mainly larch and spruce. Above the castle lies heather-dominated moorland with patches of blaeberry.

Many wild animals live in the area. Smaller but more commonly seen in the spring and summer is the mountain hare. Sometimes called the blue hare, it grows a thick white coat in the winter, for warmth and camouflage.

Red deer and roe deer are also common, but elusive. The male and female red deer live in separate herds for much of the year, coming together in the autumn to breed. Roe deer are much smaller, and tend to live individually or in small groups. They are usually found in the woodlands, but can often be seen in the early mornings feeding in the fields around the castle.

The surrounding grassland and moorland are home to many birds. One example, the snow bunting, is resident in the Cairngorms; elsewhere it is a winter visitor, returning to Scandinavia to breed during the short Arctic summer. The lapwing and skylark are also common in this area. The lapwing or peewit – so named after its distinctive display call – lives on the lower farm land and marshy valley bottom. The skylark prefers the open grassland and moorland fringe. It has a distinctive twittering call and is often heard singing high overhead on fine summer days.

Above: A flock of snow buntings at Corgarff.

Corgarff Castle is one of over 20 Historic Scotland sites in Aberdeenshire, a selection of which is shown below.

Kildrummy Castle	Huntly Castle	Tolquhon Castle	Balvenie Castle
↗ 10 miles SW of Alford on the A97	↗ In Huntly on the A96	↗ In Meigle, 6m SE of Glamis off the A94	↗ At Dufftown on the A941
🕐 Open summer only	🕐 Open all year; winter: closed Thursdays and Fridays	🕐 Open all year; winter: weekends only	🕐 Open summer only
📞 01975 571331	📞 01466 793191	📞 01651 851286	📞 01340 820121
🚗 Approx. 15 miles from Corgarff Castle	🚗 Approx. 25 miles from Corgarff Castle	🚗 Approx. 45 miles from Corgarff Castle	🚗 Approx. 30 miles from Corgarff Castle
Facilities	Facilities	Facilities	Facilities

For more information on all Historic Scotland sites, visit **www.historic-scotland.gov.uk**
To order tickets and a wide range of gifts, visit **www.historic-scotland.gov.uk/shop**

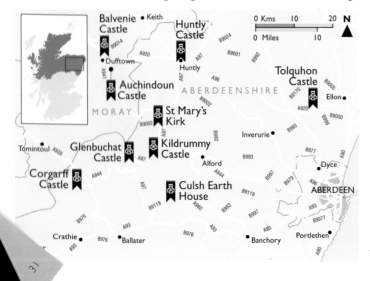

Key to facilities

Admission charge	£
Bus/coach parking	🚌
Car parking	P
Interpretive display	
Picnic area	
Reasonable wheelchair access	♿
Shop	
Cafe/restaurant	
Tea/coffee stop	
Toilets	🚻
Visitor centre	
Disabled toilets	♿
Bicycle parking	
Strong footwear recommended	